How To Get Help, Stay Safe In Public, And Protect Yourself From Bullying & Abuse

Irene van der Zande

Illustrations By Amanda Golert

Editing And Adaptations By Marylaine Léger

A Publication Of

kid**power** teen**power** full**power**®
international

Use Your Fullpower To Stay Safe, Act Wisely, And Believe In Yourself!

Copyright And Permission To Use Information

Kidpower Teenpower Fullpower International

Office 831-426-4407 or (USA) 1-800-467-6997
E-mail safety@kidpower.org
Web page www.kidpower.org
Address P.O. Box 1212, Santa Cruz, CA 95061, USA

Table Of Contents

Note: Stories for Skill Sets 1 to 6 are in the first book of this series:

Fullpower Social Safety Stories For Teens and Adults Book 1.
How To Avoid Trouble, Protect Your Emotional Safety, And Set Boundaries

Introducing The Fullpower Friends

Come join the Fullpower Friends—Mike, Rosa, Mei Lin, Talib, and Safety Officer Camilla— while they show how to use their "full power" to stay safe and have better relationships with people.

This book has examples, stories, and practices of 'People Safety' skills and ideas. 'People Safety' means making safe choices and protecting your feelings when others act thoughtless, mean, scary, or dangerous.

'People Safety' also means knowing how to stay in charge of what you say and do so that you are always acting safely and respectfully towards others, even when you feel upset.

Using 'People Safety' skills will help you to have more fun, develop positive relationships, feel more confident, and stay safe from most bullying, abuse, and other violence.

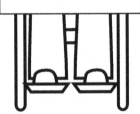

Mike loves everyone and has a great sense of humor. He worries about whether people will like him.

Mei Lin is proud of who she is and a strong advocate. Her difficulty in compromising can cause conflicts.

Talib is caring and trustworthy. His shyness about speaking up can cause others to misunderstand or ignore him.

Rosa is wise, compassionate, and confident. She can get so caught up in caring for others that she forgets to take care of herself.

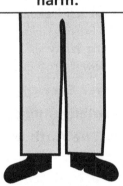

Safety Officer Camilla knows a lot about 'People Safety' and teaches people how to protect themselves from harm.

4

A publication of Kidpower Teenpower Fullpower International® www.kidpower.org
© 2017 For permission to copy, contact safety@kidpower.org

Fullpower Social Safety Stories

– Skill Set #7 –

Get Help When You Have A Safety Problem

The Friends Are At The Mall

1. Mei Lin, Rosa, Mike, and Talib all go to the shopping mall to see the stores.

A publication of Kidpower Teenpower Fullpower International® www.kidpower.org
© 2017 For permission to copy, contact safety@kidpower.org

EASY SHOPPING   TOYS

Come here you creeps!

2. Some mean people start to yell at them. They use their Walk Away Power and their Roll Away Power.

To Practice	
DO:	Move away towards Safety.
DO:	Use Mouth Closed Power.

A publication of Kidpower Teenpower Fullpower International® www.kidpower.org

3. The Fullpower friends follow their Safety Plan and go into the clothing store to get help.

A publication of Kidpower Teenpower Fullpower International® www.kidpower.org
© 2017 For permission to copy, contact safety@kidpower.org

4. The friends ask for help, but the store clerk does not want to get involved.

To Practice

DO: Go to a person in charge.

SAY: We need help.

A publication of Kidpower Teenpower Fullpower International® www.kidpower.org
© 2017 For permission to copy, contact safety@kidpower.org

5. The friends keep asking, but the store clerk tells them to get out of the store.

To Practice

DO: Stay calm and confident.

SAY: We have a Safety Problem.

A publication of Kidpower Teenpower Fullpower International® www.kidpower.org
© 2017 For permission to copy, contact safety@kidpower.org

6. Because it is not safe to leave the store, the friends persist in asking the store clerk to help them. Persist or persistent means not giving up. When people who are supposed to help do not listen, sometimes you have to be very firm.

To Practice
DO: Stay calm and persistent.
SAY: Please call security.

11

Rosa Tells To Get Help

1. If you have a Safety Problem, get help from an adult you trust as quickly as you can. Keep asking until you get the help you need. After Rosa gets away from Abel, who has crossed the line with her, Rosa decides that the person who can help her the most is her mother.

A publication of Kidpower Teenpower Fullpower International® www.kidpower.org
© 2017 For permission to copy, contact safety@kidpower.org

2. Rosa tells her mother that she has a problem. Her mother is busy on the computer and does not understand what Rosa says.

To Practice

DO: Go to a person in charge. Use a calm, clear voice.

SAY: Excuse me. I have a Safety Problem.

13

A publication of Kidpower Teenpower Fullpower International® www.kidpower.org
© 2017 For permission to copy, contact safety@kidpower.org

3. Rosa asks her mother to listen to her. Her mother has had a hard day and gets angry.

To Practice

DO: Stay calm and persistent. Use a flat, calm hand to touch their arm.

SAY: Please listen to me!

4. Rosa knows that it is okay to interrupt her mother and keep asking for help if she has a Safety Problem.

To Practice

DO: Stay calm and persistent.

SAY: I have a Safety Problem.

A publication of Kidpower Teenpower Fullpower International® www.kidpower.org
© 2017 For permission to copy, contact safety@kidpower.org

5. Rosa tells her mother that Abel did not listen. But her mother does not understand. Rosa's mother cannot read Rosa's mind.

To Practice

DO: Take a breath to stay calm.

SAY: This is about safety!

A publication of Kidpower Teenpower Fullpower International® www.kidpower.org
© 2017 For permission to copy, contact safety@kidpower.org

But, wait there's more! He wanted to hold my hand, and I told him to stop. He didn't listen, and then he tried to bribe me. He got angry and told me not to tell.

Thank you for telling me. I'm sorry I yelled at you. We will figure out what to do.

6. Rosa tells her mom the whole story. Her mother will help her.

To Practice

DO: Stay persistent.

SAY: Wait. There's more.

17

A publication of Kidpower Teenpower Fullpower International® www.kidpower.org
© 2017 For permission to copy, contact safety@kidpower.org

Talib Keeps Asking Until He Gets Help

1. Talib is walking to the bus stop at school. Another student starts to bully him by grabbing his backpack.

2. Talib uses his Stop Power and yells "NO". He uses his Walk Away Power to go find a safer place to be.

To Practice

DO: Make a stop sign with your hands and use a strong, firm voice.

SAY: Yell 'NO!' from your belly.

A publication of Kidpower Teenpower Fullpower International® www.kidpower.org
© 2017 For permission to copy, contact safety@kidpower.org

3. The student bullying Talib keeps following him and saying cruel things. Talib protects his feelings.

To Practice

DO: Use your Imagination Trash Can to throw away the hurting words.

SAY: (to yourself) I am powerful.

DO: Leave calmly, quietly, and quickly.

4. Talib goes to the principal's office for help but the principal is too busy to listen.

A publication of Kidpower Teenpower Fullpower International® www.kidpower.org
© 2017 For permission to copy, contact safety@kidpower.org

5. Talib goes to the janitor, but today she is very busy and having a bad day.

To Practice

DO: Sit or stand tall. Use a calm, firm voice.

SAY: Excuse me. I need your help.

A publication of Kidpower Teenpower Fullpower International® www.kidpower.org
© 2017 For permission to copy, contact safety@kidpower.org

He is trying to grab my backpack. He said he can do anything he wants because I can't see... but I can HEAR him!

I am glad you told me. I will help you.

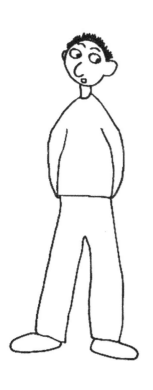

6. Talib meets his favorite teacher in the hall and gets help so he can be safe.

To Practice

DO: Keep asking until you get the help you need.

SAY: This is about safety. I need help.

23

A publication of Kidpower Teenpower Fullpower International® www.kidpower.org
© 2017 For permission to copy, contact safety@kidpower.org

Fullpower Social Safety Stories

– Skill Set #8 –

Stay Safe With Touch And Private Areas

Protect Safety With Touch When Rules Are Broken

If you are about to hit somebody, being stopped is not a choice. If you are badly hurt, you may have to go to the doctor.

1. Touch for health and safety is often not a choice. But any kind of touch as well as games, problems, photos, presents someone gives you, and activities should not have to be a secret.

To Practice

SAY: <u>Touch</u> should not be a secret. <u>Presents someone gives you</u> should not be a secret. <u>Videos or photos</u> should not be a secret. <u>Friendships</u> should not be a secret. <u>Games or activities</u> should not be a secret.

A publication of Kidpower Teenpower Fullpower International® www.kidpower.org

Problems should not be secrets. Any kind of touch that bothers you should **not** have to be a secret.

2. Touch of any kind should never ever have to be a secret — whether you like it or not and whether it is a choice or not.

___To Practice___

SAY: Problems should not be secrets.

Stop or else!

3. Suppose someone crosses and breaks the safety rules. You can say, "Stop or else!". And you can add "...I will leave!" or, "...You have to leave!" or, "...I'll report you!"

To Practice

DO: Use a firm voice and confident body.

SAY: Stop or I will leave!

27

If someone offers you an unsafe bribe, they are breaking the safety rules.

You can say, "Stop or I will leave," or, "Stop or you will have to leave," or, "Stop or I will tell."

Stop or I will tell!

4. An unsafe bribe is when someone tries to give you something to get you to lower your boundaries and do something unsafe, dishonest, or unkind.

To Practice

DO: Use a firm voice and confident body.

SAY: Stop or you will have to leave!

A publication of Kidpower Teenpower Fullpower International® www.kidpower.org
© 2017 For permission to copy, contact safety@kidpower.org

5. If someone tries to force you to do something that you know is wrong, they are breaking the safety rules.

To Practice

DO:	Use a firm voice and confident body.
SAY:	Stop or I will report you!

A publication of Kidpower Teenpower Fullpower International® www.kidpower.org
© 2017 For permission to copy, contact safety@kidpower.org

Another way of breaking the safety rules about touch is breaking the safety rules about private areas.

6. Private areas are the parts of people's bodies that can be covered by a bathing suit.

A publication of Kidpower Teenpower Fullpower International® www.kidpower.org
© 2017 For permission to copy, contact safety@kidpower.org

7. The safety rules are that, except for health or safety, other people should not try to touch or look at your private areas, or try to get you to touch or look at their private areas.

They should not make or show you videos or photos about you or others and their private areas.

To Practice

DO: Make a wall with your hands.

SAY: Stop or I will tell!

31

A publication of Kidpower Teenpower Fullpower International® www.kidpower.org
© 2017 For permission to copy, contact safety@kidpower.org

What if a person is a grown-up or a teenager?

The rules are different in different homes. Sexual relationships take a lot of responsibility and should never have to be a secret.

8. As you grow up, the safety rules about touching private areas can change. Talk with your families or adult support people about your rules and values.

The Too-Long Kiss

1. Talib and his girlfriend Mira love each other. How long, how often, and when to kiss is often different for different people, even when they care about each other.

2. Talib really likes kissing Mira.

A publication of Kidpower Teenpower Fullpower International® www.kidpower.org
© 2017 For permission to copy, contact safety@kidpower.org

3. Mira doesn't like long kisses in public.

To Practice

SAY: Not right now.

A publication of Kidpower Teenpower Fullpower International®   www.kidpower.org
© 2017   For permission to copy, contact safety@kidpower.org

4. Talib's feelings get hurt. Mira explains what she likes and doesn't like. Affection has to be okay with each person, even when two people are a couple.

To Practice

SAY: Kisses have to be okay with both people.

SAY: Thank you for telling me.

A publication of Kidpower Teenpower Fullpower International® www.kidpower.org
© 2017 For permission to copy, contact safety@kidpower.org

The Uncomfortable Photos

1. Rosa's cousin Joanna loves taking photos. Rosa doesn't enjoy it very much. She is thinking that she should speak up and tell Joanna that it bothers her.

A publication of Kidpower Teenpower Fullpower International® www.kidpower.org
© 2017 For permission to copy, contact safety@kidpower.org

2. After Joanna takes a photo when she is coming out of the shower, Rosa has had enough! She uses Speak Up Power to let her know.

To Practice

DO: Make a wall with your hands. Use a strong, firm voice.

SAY: STOP!

A publication of Kidpower Teenpower Fullpower International® www.kidpower.org
© 2017 For permission to copy, contact safety@kidpower.org

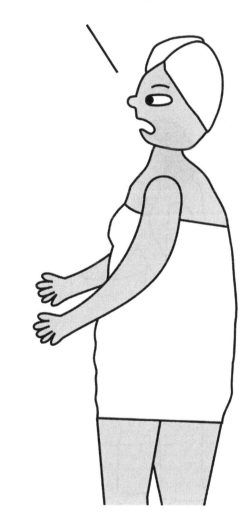

3. Joanna gets upset and tries to make Rosa feel wrong for setting a boundary.

To Practice

DO: Use a calm voice and confident body.

SAY: I care about you AND I want you to stop.

SAY: Stop or I will leave!

I am part of your family, and you are not being very respectful.

Safety means that family members respect each other's privacy. You sent that picture of me to all your friends even though I told you not to.

4. Joanna does not respect Rosa's wishes so Rosa leaves.

A publication of Kidpower Teenpower Fullpower International® www.kidpower.org
© 2017 For permission to copy, contact safety@kidpower.org

Ensuring Consent Can Be Romantic

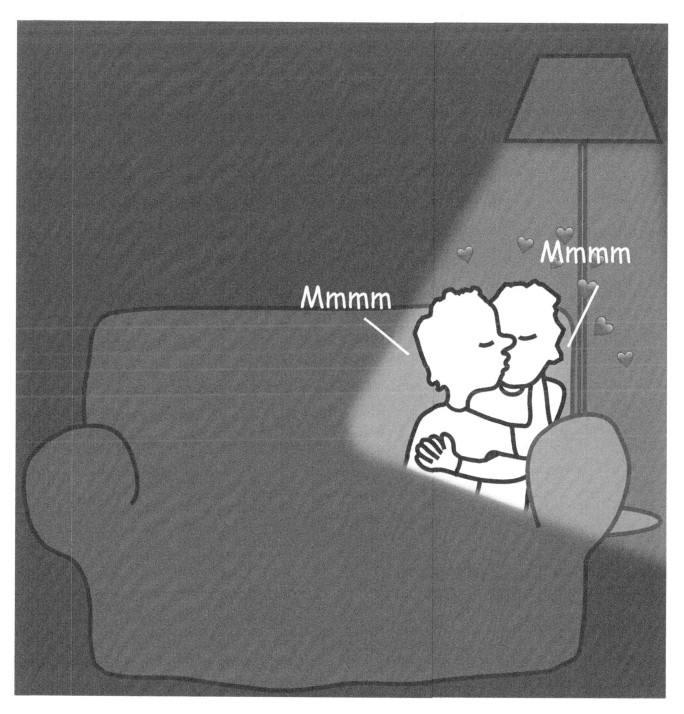

1. As long as it follows the safety rules (by being safe, not a secret, allowed by the adults in charge, and okay with both), touching each other can give lots of pleasure.

A publication of Kidpower Teenpower Fullpower International® www.kidpower.org
© 2017 For permission to copy, contact safety@kidpower.org

2. Each person needs to speak up about what DOES and does NOT feel good to them.

To Practice

SAY: We each belong to ourselves.

SAY: Affection & touch needs to be OK with both.

A publication of Kidpower Teenpower Fullpower International® www.kidpower.org
© 2017 For permission to copy, contact safety@kidpower.org

3. It's important to Check First to make sure both of you are okay.

To Practice

SAY: Check First.

SAY: Touch must stay OK with both.

A publication of Kidpower Teenpower Fullpower International® www.kidpower.org
© 2017 For permission to copy, contact safety@kidpower.org

4. It's okay to like something for a while and then to change your mind. To stay safe, romantic touch needs to continue to be truly okay with each person, and stop as soon as someone changes their mind.

To Practice

SAY: Each person can change their mind.

SAY: I don't like that anymore. Please stop.

A publication of Kidpower Teenpower Fullpower International® www.kidpower.org
© 2017 For permission to copy, contact safety@kidpower.org

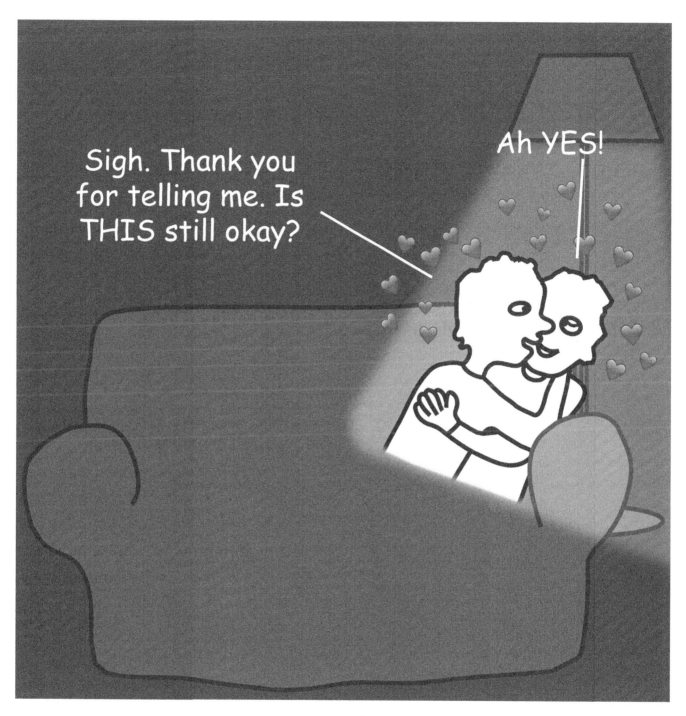

5. When you check with each other and speak up, you can stay safe and have more fun.

To Practice

SAY: Check & check again.

SAY: Speak up to stay safe.

SAY: Thank you for telling me.

A publication of Kidpower Teenpower Fullpower International® www.kidpower.org
© 2017 For permission to copy, contact safety@kidpower.org

People can NOT give consent if they are scared, drugged, drunk, asleep, tricked, or emotionally pressured.
Only do things that BOTH people feel good about doing.

6. Consent means freely choosing to say "Yes" and always feeling okay to say "No" to any kind of sexual behavior or to change your mind about it. If you see someone who is breaking the safety rules about this, speak up if it is safe to do so or leave and get help.

To Practice

SAY: That's not safe!

A publication of Kidpower Teenpower Fullpower International® www.kidpower.org
© 2017 For permission to copy, contact safety@kidpower.org

Fullpower Social Safety Stories

– Skill Set #9 –

Stay Safe With Strangers And In Public

Friends At The Park

A stranger is just someone we don't know well. Here at the park, we are strangers to these people, and they are strangers to us. Most people are good even if we don't know each other.

I'm afraid of strangers!

Stranger Danger!

If I see a stranger, I am going to hit him before he hits me!

1. People you see all the time can still be strangers or acquaintances, so they are not people you know well. It is normal to have scary pictures in our minds about strangers.

A publication of Kidpower Teenpower Fullpower International® www.kidpower.org
© 2017 For permission to copy, contact safety@kidpower.org

We see that clown here all the time. He is nice to kids. Is he still a stranger?

The clown seems really nice but no one here knows him really well.

It is OK for those kids to get balloons from him because they are with their adults, but not to go somewhere else with him.

2. Even familiar, interesting, or friendly people can still be strangers.

A publication of Kidpower Teenpower Fullpower International® www.kidpower.org
© 2017 For permission to copy, contact safety@kidpower.org

It takes both time and information to get to know someone.
Do we know where people live? Their names?
Their friends or family?
Where they work or go to school?

So when does somebody stop being a stranger and start being somebody we know?

3. Knowing when to stop treating someone like a stranger is complicated.

A publication of Kidpower Teenpower Fullpower International® www.kidpower.org
© 2017 For permission to copy, contact safety@kidpower.org

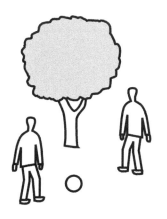

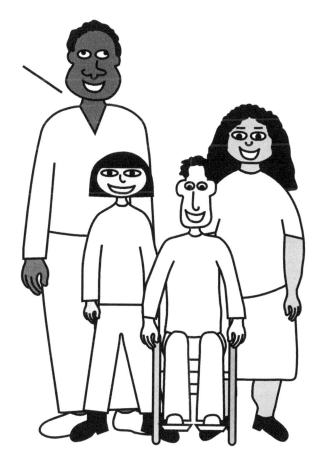

We don't need to be afraid of strangers. We just need to remember how to be safe with strangers.

4. The Fullpower Friends have a great time at the park. They know they can make Safety Plans for when they need to go places and be with people they don't know well. They can let people who care about them know where they are and who they are with before changing their plans.

To Practice

SAY: Make a Safety Plan for Everywhere I go.

51

A publication of Kidpower Teenpower Fullpower International® www.kidpower.org
© 2017 For permission to copy, contact safety@kidpower.org

Rosa Keeps Herself Safe On The Bus

1. Rosa likes to ride the bus. She says hello to lots of nice people.

A publication of Kidpower Teenpower Fullpower International® www.kidpower.org
© 2017 For permission to copy, contact safety@kidpower.org

2. A drunk guy gets on the bus. He sits next to Rosa. Rosa ignores him. The drunk guy touches Rosa's hair. She yells at him and pushes his hand away.

To Practice

DO: Use your own hand to remove someone's hand away. Use a firm, loud voice.
SAY: NO! STOP!

A publication of Kidpower Teenpower Fullpower International® www.kidpower.org
© 2017 For permission to copy, contact safety@kidpower.org

3. Rosa yells for help. She says that the man is bothering her. Everybody on the bus yells at the drunk guy. He is in trouble.

To Practice

DO: Make your body tall. Use a loud voice to attract attention.

SAY: I NEED HELP!

4. As soon as she can, Rosa walks to the front of the bus. She tells the driver about the drunk guy.

To Practice

DO:	Move towards a person in charge.
SAY:	Excuse me. I need help.

A publication of Kidpower Teenpower Fullpower International® www.kidpower.org
© 2017 For permission to copy, contact safety@kidpower.org

5. The driver makes the drunk guy get off the bus. It is against the rules to bother people on the bus.

A publication of Kidpower Teenpower Fullpower International® www.kidpower.org
© 2017 For permission to copy, contact safety@kidpower.org

6. Rosa is proud of herself for making the drunk guy stop bothering her. She feels safe because the driver made the drunk guy get off the bus.

A publication of Kidpower Teenpower Fullpower International® www.kidpower.org
© 2017 For permission to copy, contact safety@kidpower.org

Rosa Uses An Emergency Lie

1. Rosa doesn't have to tell the truth to someone who has been acting threatening. Rosa's job is to get away from this person as soon as she can to avoid a Safety Problem for herself.

A publication of Kidpower Teenpower Fullpower International® www.kidpower.org
© 2017 For permission to copy, contact safety@kidpower.org

To Practice

DO: Make your body tall. Use a calm, firm voice.

SAY: Sorry! I am with someone else.

A publication of Kidpower Teenpower Fullpower International® www.kidpower.org
© 2017 For permission to copy, contact safety@kidpower.org

Staying Safe Online

1. Online technology is great because it can make communication easier.

A publication of Kidpower Teenpower Fullpower International® www.kidpower.org
© 2017 For permission to copy, contact safety@kidpower.org

2. The people you meet on the Internet are strangers to you. Check and Think First before you give out personal information, even on semi-secure sites like YouTube & Facebook. Make a Safety Plan before you meet or talk to anyone you get to know via the Internet.

To Practice

SAY: Make a Safety Plan for going online.

SAY: Check First before changing the plan.

61

A publication of Kidpower Teenpower Fullpower International® www.kidpower.org
© 2017 For permission to copy, contact safety@kidpower.org

2. The people you meet on the Internet are strangers to you. Check and Think First before you give out personal information. The Internet is a great way to learn many things, but not everything you find on it is true. Double-check the source on any sites to make sure you are getting accurate information.

To Practice
SAY: Think First!

A publication of Kidpower Teenpower Fullpower International® www.kidpower.org
© 2017 For permission to copy, contact safety@kidpower.org

4. Some sites on the Internet may be against the rules of your school, workplace, organization, or family.

To Practice

SAY: Move away!

DO: Click to turn off or leave.

A publication of Kidpower Teenpower Fullpower International®   www.kidpower.org
© 2017   For permission to copy, contact safety@kidpower.org

Fullpower Social Safety Stories

– Skill Set #10 –

Be Powerful With Your Voice And Body

A publication of Kidpower Teenpower Fullpower International® www.kidpower.org
© 2017 For permission to copy, contact safety@kidpower.org

Yelling For Safety STOP! I NEED HELP!

1. If someone is scaring you or acting unsafely, you can tell this person to STOP! You can quickly leave and go get help. A guy who bullies others at school says he is going to beat Mike up. Mike yells "STOP!" and makes a wall with his hands.

To Practice

DO: Make a wall with your hands.

SAY: STOP! with a loud, firm voice.

65

A publication of Kidpower Teenpower Fullpower International® www.kidpower.org

2. Mike hurries to his teacher for help. She will help him.

To Practice
SAY: (in a strong loud voice) I NEED HELP!
DO: Leave and go to safety.

3. A woman at work is mad at Rosa. She uses rude words and acts scary. Rosa yells, "STOP!" and makes a wall with her hands. The woman stops and Rosa leaves.

To Practice

DO: Make a wall with your hands.

SAY: STOP! with a loud, firm voice.

A publication of Kidpower Teenpower Fullpower International®   www.kidpower.org

4. Rosa hurries to her boss for help. He says he will help her.

To Practice
SAY: I need help!
SAY: I have a Safety Problem.

A publication of Kidpower Teenpower Fullpower International® www.kidpower.org

5. A growling dog near Mei Lin's house scares her. She yells "STOP!" and makes a wall with her hands.

To Practice
DO: Make a wall with your hands.
SAY: STOP! with a loud, firm voice.

A publication of Kidpower Teenpower Fullpower International®   www.kidpower.org
© 2017   For permission to copy, contact safety@kidpower.org

6. Mei Lin goes to her neighbor for help. He says he will help her.

To Practice

SAY: I need help!

SAY: I have a Safety Problem.

7. A mean guy on the street acts like he is going to hurt Talib. Talib yells "STOP!" He makes a wall with one hand and holds onto his cane with the other hand. The mean guy stops and Talib leaves.

To Practice

DO: Make a wall with your hands.

SAY: STOP! with a loud, firm voice.

71

8. Talib hurries to a police officer for help. The police officer says that he will help Talib.

To Practice
SAY: I need help!
SAY: I have a Safety Problem.

Talib Goes From Cower To Power

1. The woman is yelling. Talib puts his head down. The woman feels like she can get him so she yells more.

To Practice

SAY: Not safe.

A publication of Kidpower Teenpower Fullpower International® www.kidpower.org
© 2017 For permission to copy, contact safety@kidpower.org

2. The woman yells and Talib yells back. This makes her yell more. Then he yells more. They are stuck yelling at each other.

3. Talib remembers his Walk Away Power. The woman yells but this time Talib leaves politely. He stays aware and confident, even when he leaves. The woman will probably leave him alone.

To Practice

DO: Move away calmly. Stay aware and confident. Use a calm voice.

SAY: Have a nice day!

75

A publication of Kidpower Teenpower Fullpower International® www.kidpower.org

4. The woman yells at Talib when he is in a corner and cannot just leave. Talib remembers his Stop Power using his voice and his hands. Then Talib leaves to go get help.

To Practice

DO: Make a wall with your hands. Make your body tall.

SAY: STOP! ... LEAVE! .... HELP!

A publication of Kidpower Teenpower Fullpower International® www.kidpower.org
© 2017 For permission to copy, contact safety@kidpower.org

Mei Lin Gets Away From Trouble

1. The Arm Grab Escape can help you get away from someone who is grabbing you without having to hurt that person. Mei Lin is walking home. There are some men who are whistling at her and making comments about how she looks.

To Practice	
DO:	Use your Mouth Closed Power.
DO:	Stay aware and act confident.

77

2. One of the guys grabs her arm even if she tries to stay out of reach.

A publication of Kidpower Teenpower Fullpower International®   www.kidpower.org
© 2017 For permission to copy, contact safety@kidpower.org

3. Mei Lin grabs her own arm, and pulls away, yelling, "NO!" The guys who are bothering her are very surprised! She walks away quickly with awareness.

To Practice

DO: Grab your own hand. Pull it away with your whole body.

SAY: Yell NO! loudly and firmly.

A publication of Kidpower Teenpower Fullpower International® www.kidpower.org
© 2017 For permission to copy, contact safety@kidpower.org

4. Mei Lin is going to tell her mother what happened right away.

To Practice

DO: Move away with calm confidence and awareness.

A publication of Kidpower Teenpower Fullpower International® www.kidpower.org
© 2017 For permission to copy, contact safety@kidpower.org

Mike Uses An Emergency Lie

1. Mike chooses to lie to help protect someone who is being threatened and to also keep himself safe.

A publication of Kidpower Teenpower Fullpower International® www.kidpower.org
© 2017 For permission to copy, contact safety@kidpower.org

2. Mike's job is to get away from these people and report the problem as soon as he can to someone who can help.

To Practice

DO: Stay out of reach.

SAY: (Yell) 'THE POLICE ARE COMING!'

A publication of Kidpower Teenpower Fullpower International® www.kidpower.org
© 2017 For permission to copy, contact safety@kidpower.org

Fullpower Social Safety Stories

– Skill Set #11 –

Stop Bullying By Taking Charge Of Safety

A publication of Kidpower Teenpower Fullpower International® www.kidpower.org
© 2017 For permission to copy, contact safety@kidpower.org

What's Bullying? What To Do About It?

1. Safety Officer Camilla explains that bullying can make people very unhappy. We all have the right to be safe and respected — and the responsibility to act safely and respectfully towards ourselves and others.

A publication of Kidpower Teenpower Fullpower International® www.kidpower.org
© 2017 For permission to copy, contact safety@kidpower.org

You can use your 'People Safety' skills to protect yourself from bullying. First, find friends and adults who can help you.

2. Pushing, shoving, or laughing in an unkind way at someone is bullying.

A publication of Kidpower Teenpower Fullpower International® www.kidpower.org
© 2017 For permission to copy, contact safety@kidpower.org

3. Threatening to hurt someone is bullying.

4. Mike makes a Safety Plan for himself. He leaves and then asks for help from his teacher.

A publication of Kidpower Teenpower Fullpower International® www.kidpower.org
© 2017 For permission to copy, contact safety@kidpower.org

5. Tripping, shoving or laughing at someone is bullying.

4. Talib can get his balance, move away, set a boundary and leave.

To Practice

DO: Make a wall with your hands. Make your body tall.

SAY: STOP! ... I'm leaving.

A publication of Kidpower Teenpower Fullpower International® www.kidpower.org
© 2017 For permission to copy, contact safety@kidpower.org

Take Charge To Stay Safe From Bullying

1. Leaving someone out is bullying.

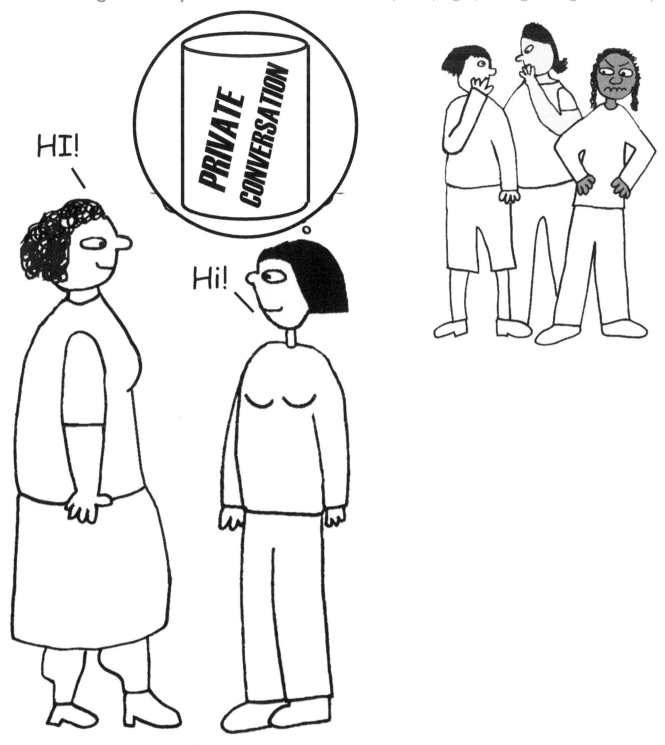

2. Mei Lin can find someone else to talk to.

To Practice

DO: Throw hurting words in your Imagination Trash Can.

SAY: (to yourself) I will find a kind person to talk with.

3. Trying to make other people not like someone is bullying. A girl at school is making up lies about Rosa.

A publication of Kidpower Teenpower Fullpower International® www.kidpower.org
© 2017 For permission to copy, contact safety@kidpower.org

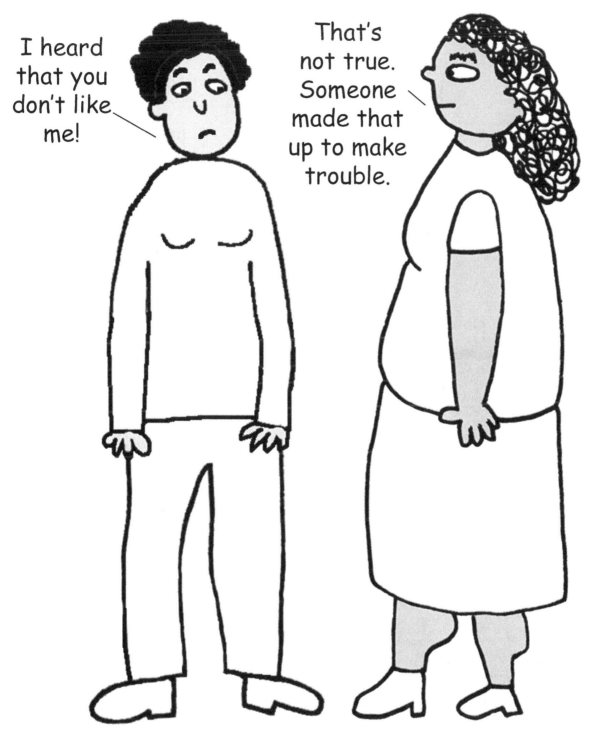

4. If someone says bad things about her, Rosa can speak up for herself.

To Practice
DO: Use a calm voice.
SAY: That's not true. Someone's making it up.

93

A publication of Kidpower Teenpower Fullpower International® www.kidpower.org
© 2017 For permission to copy, contact safety@kidpower.org

4. Making fun of people is bullying. Some students are making mean jokes about Mike and Mei Lin.

A publication of Kidpower Teenpower Fullpower International® www.kidpower.org
© 2017 For permission to copy, contact safety@kidpower.org

5. Mike and Mei Lin can throw away hurtful words and say something nice to themselves. They can leave. If people keep bothering them, they can get help.

To Practice

DO: Throw the hurtful words away.

SAY: I like myself.

A publication of Kidpower Teenpower Fullpower International® www.kidpower.org
© 2017 For permission to copy, contact safety@kidpower.org

Talib Gets Bullied At Work

1. There is a guy at work named JoJo who lots of people like. Talib does not like JoJo because JoJo is always picking on him and calling him names.

A publication of Kidpower Teenpower Fullpower International® www.kidpower.org
© 2017 For permission to copy, contact safety@kidpower.org

2. JoJo is always poking Talib and putting him down. If someone is picking on you and calling you names, it is normal to feel alone and like it is your fault.

A publication of Kidpower Teenpower Fullpower International® www.kidpower.org
© 2017 For permission to copy, contact safety@kidpower.org

3. In the lunch room, JoJo knocks Talib's tray over on purpose.

A publication of Kidpower Teenpower Fullpower International® www.kidpower.org
© 2017 For permission to copy, contact safety@kidpower.org

4. JoJo tells Talib that he will get him fired and beat him up if he tells. Talib promised not to tell.

A publication of Kidpower Teenpower Fullpower International® www.kidpower.org
© 2017 For permission to copy, contact safety@kidpower.org

5. Talib tells his friends what is happening at work. They feel bad for him.

To Practice

SAY: Problems should not be secrets.

A publication of Kidpower Teenpower Fullpower International® www.kidpower.org

6. Two of Talib's colleagues talk to him. They help him to be safe at work. If you know someone is being bullied at work, at school, or in your community, speak up if you can do so safely — and reach out to offer your support.

A publication of Kidpower Teenpower Fullpower International® www.kidpower.org
© 2017 For permission to copy, contact safety@kidpower.org

7. Next time JoJo tries to bother Talib at work, Talib interrupts and tells him to stop. Then Talib uses his Walk Away Power and leaves.

To Practice

DO: Use a calm, firm voice and interrupt.

SAY: STOP! I AM LEAVING!

8. Talib's friends help him tell the whole story to their supervisor so that he will understand the problem.

To Practice

SAY: Get help.

SAY: Be persistent. Don't give up.

A publication of Kidpower Teenpower Fullpower International® www.kidpower.org
© 2017 For permission to copy, contact safety@kidpower.org

Stop Others From Bullying

We can work together to create caring, respect, and safety for everyone, everywhere.

1. Don't agree with hurtful teasing or jokes. Tell people to respect differences.

To Practice
DO: Use a calm, firm voice and interrupt.
SAY: That's not funny. That's prejudice.

A publication of Kidpower Teenpower Fullpower International® www.kidpower.org

Hi. How's it going? I am sorry those other girls were mean to you.

Thank you!

2. If someone is being left out, go talk with that person.

To Practice

DO: Reach out to someone who was bullied.

SAY: I am sorry that happened. Let's get help.

A publication of Kidpower Teenpower Fullpower International® www.kidpower.org

3. If someone is being hurt or threatened, speak up if you can do it safely.

To Practice

DO: Use a calm, firm voice and interrupt.

SAY: STOP! That's against the rules here.

A publication of Kidpower Teenpower Fullpower International® www.kidpower.org
© 2017 For permission to copy, contact safety@kidpower.org

4. If someone tries to make you feel bad about someone else, ask why and say that you don't listen to gossip.

To Practice

DO: Use a calm, firm voice and interrupt.

SAY: I won't believe it unless they tell me.

107

5. People should be safe at school, at work, at home, and in their communities. Report problems like people being hurt, threatened, made fun of, or left out.

A publication of Kidpower Teenpower Fullpower International® www.kidpower.org
© 2017 For permission to copy, contact safety@kidpower.org

Mike Takes Charge

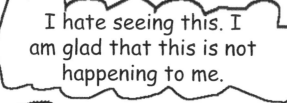

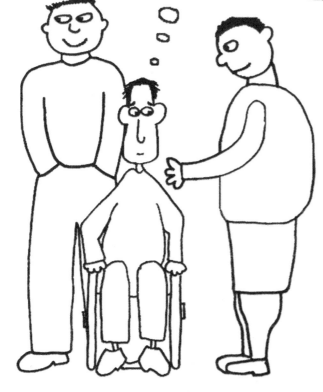

1. Mike is talking with some friends. He notices that some kids are bullying a smaller guy. He feels guilty and sad.

A publication of Kidpower Teenpower Fullpower International® www.kidpower.org

LOOK OUT! RUN! A TEACHER IS COMING!

Everybody better shut up about this unless you want some of THIS!

2. Mike does not want to have the bullies bother him, but he does want to help the smaller guy. He pretends to see a teacher coming so that the bullies will leave.

To Practice

DO: Stay out of reach. Use a loud voice and interrupt.

SAY: RUN! A TEACHER IS COMING!

3. Mike reaches out to support the smaller guy, who introduces himself.

To Practice

SAY: I am sad that happened.

A publication of Kidpower Teenpower Fullpower International® www.kidpower.org
© 2017 For permission to copy, contact safety@kidpower.org

4. Mike tells Frank that they need to get help. Frank is afraid. He does not want the bullies to take revenge on them for telling.

___ **To Practice** ___

SAY: Get help for a Safety Problem.

A publication of Kidpower Teenpower Fullpower International® www.kidpower.org
© 2017 For permission to copy, contact safety@kidpower.org

5. Mike says that the bullies will bother Frank and other people again if they are not stopped. Frank is worried but he agrees.

A publication of Kidpower Teenpower Fullpower International® www.kidpower.org
© 2017 For permission to copy, contact safety@kidpower.org

6. Mike and Frank talk to Mike's favorite teacher at school. She promises to let the bullies think that she saw what happened so they won't know that Mike and Frank told. She is glad that they came to her for help.

A publication of Kidpower Teenpower Fullpower International® www.kidpower.org
© 2017 For permission to copy, contact safety@kidpower.org

Prevent Cyberbullying

Cyberbullying happens when people use technology to be hurtful to someone such as mobile phones, chat rooms, gaming environments, and social media.

1. Don't post or write anything on the Internet that you don't want the world to see. This is true for e-mails, social networks, and instant messages as well as text messages and digital photos on mobile phones. You want to be very careful what you write, say, and do, as it can get passed around to lots of people quickly.

A publication of Kidpower Teenpower Fullpower International® www.kidpower.org
© 2017 For permission to copy, contact safety@kidpower.org

2. When people misuse technology to bully others, it is called cyberbullying. Cyberbullying is against the law. Think about whether what you are doing might be hurtful or embarrassing to someone.

To Practice

SAY: Think First.

A publication of Kidpower Teenpower Fullpower International® www.kidpower.org
© 2017 For permission to copy, contact safety@kidpower.org

3. Speak up if you see anyone cyberbullying and tell them that it is wrong. Get help from other people you trust, if you need to.

To Practice

SAY: Please stop. That is an unkind thing to do.

117

A publication of Kidpower Teenpower Fullpower International® www.kidpower.org
© 2017 For permission to copy, contact safety@kidpower.org

OH NO! That guy from the soccer game is really mad at me. He is saying he is going to tell everyone horrible things about me.

Save the e-mail and don't write back. We can talk to our parents and coach about what happened. And if things get worse, we can tell Safety Officer Camilla.

4. If someone does bully you over the Internet or with a text message or photo on a mobile phone, don't delete the message. Save it, print it if you can, don't reply, and get help to report what happened!

A publication of Kidpower Teenpower Fullpower International® www.kidpower.org
© 2017 For permission to copy, contact safety@kidpower.org

Rosa Gets Cyberbullied By Her Cousin

1. Rosa is shocked by the unkind messages and embarrassing photos that Joanna is texting.

A publication of Kidpower Teenpower Fullpower International® www.kidpower.org
© 2017 For permission to copy, contact safety@kidpower.org

2. Rosa tells her to stop, but Joanna does not listen.

To Practice

DO: Pretend to type on a device.

SAY: That's not OK with me. Stop.

A publication of Kidpower Teenpower Fullpower International® www.kidpower.org
© 2017 For permission to copy, contact safety@kidpower.org

3. Rosa asks her aunt for help.

To Practice

SAY: Excuse me! I have a Safety Problem.

4. Her aunt decides to stop paying for Joanna's mobile phone until she apologizes.

A publication of Kidpower Teenpower Fullpower International® www.kidpower.org
© 2017 For permission to copy, contact safety@kidpower.org

Rosa & Anna Stand-Up Against Prejudice

You two are perfect for each other!

1. Rosa and her girlfriend, Anna, love each other.

2. Sometimes people say mean things because Rosa and Anna are two women who love each other.

A publication of Kidpower Teenpower Fullpower International® www.kidpower.org
© 2017 For permission to copy, contact safety@kidpower.org

3. Rosa and Anna decide to walk away and get the bus from another bus stop. Being cruel to people for being different is unsafe and disrespectful.

To Practice

SAY: Move away to Safety.

A publication of Kidpower Teenpower Fullpower International® www.kidpower.org
© 2017 For permission to copy, contact safety@kidpower.org

No, thank you.

BUS STOP

4. Rosa speaks up in a respectful way while leaving with Anna to go to safety.

To Practice

DO: Use a calm voice while moving away with awareness.

SAY: No, thank you!

5. Rosa and Anna go to the office to report what happened.

A publication of Kidpower Teenpower Fullpower International®   www.kidpower.org
© 2017   For permission to copy, contact safety@kidpower.org

6. The woman in the office is very rude.

To Practice

DO: Throw hurting words in your Imagination Trash Can.

SAY: I am proud of who I am.

7. Rosa and Anna tell their friends what happened. Their friends are very supportive and help them.

A publication of Kidpower Teenpower Fullpower International® www.kidpower.org
© 2017 For permission to copy, contact safety@kidpower.org

I am so sorry that happened to you. Mei Lin is right. We need to teach people here that it is not okay to say mean things about other people or threaten them FOR ANY REASON.

DIRECTOR

8. They all go to the director and tell her what happened. She listens, understands, and makes a plan.

To Practice

SAY: Keep asking until you get help.

Fullpower Social Safety Stories

– Skill Set #12 –

Use
Your Fullpower
To Solve Problems

The Break-Up Story

1. Mike wants to break up with Reba, but he doesn't know how to do it. His friends tell him that he has to tell her even though she will be upset.

2. Mike tells Reba as kindly and clearly as he can, but she is still very sad. Breaking up breaks hearts. It is really hard to do.

To Practice

DO: Use a calm voice.

SAY: I think you're great AND this relationship isn't working for me.

133

A publication of Kidpower Teenpower Fullpower International® www.kidpower.org
© 2017 For permission to copy, contact safety@kidpower.org

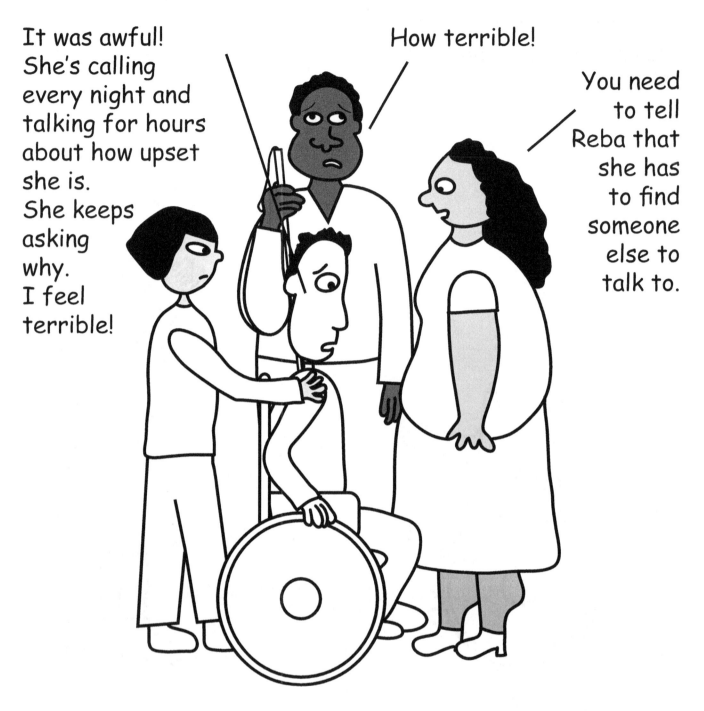

It was awful! She's calling every night and talking for hours about how upset she is. She keeps asking why. I feel terrible!

How terrible!

You need to tell Reba that she has to find someone else to talk to.

3. Mike wants Reba to be happy, but he cannot be the one to help her.

4. Sometimes the best way to help someone is to help them think of others who can help.

A publication of Kidpower Teenpower Fullpower International® www.kidpower.org
© 2017 For permission to copy, contact safety@kidpower.org

To Practice

DO: Use a calm voice.

SAY: I understand AND I can't help you.

I like both Mike and Reba and want to stay friends with both of them.

You can be friends with both but need to see them at different times and places. And not to talk about either of them to each other so that you don't get in the middle.

5. Mei Lin can stay friends with both Mike and Reba as long as she sees them separately and stays out of the middle.

A publication of Kidpower Teenpower Fullpower International® www.kidpower.org
© 2017 For permission to copy, contact safety@kidpower.org

6. Reba decides to find other people to have fun with. She misses Mike but understands that being a couple has to work well for both people.

A publication of Kidpower Teenpower Fullpower International®   www.kidpower.org
© 2017 For permission to copy, contact safety@kidpower.org

Mike Has Trouble At Home

1. Mike's mother gets into fights with her boyfriend when they are drinking. Mike is sad when they are fighting.

2. Mike's mother gets knocked down by her boyfriend. Mike is scared that she will get hurt.

A publication of Kidpower Teenpower Fullpower International®   www.kidpower.org
© 2017   For permission to copy, contact safety@kidpower.org

3. Mike tries to protect his mother. She is mad and says mean things to him.

A publication of Kidpower Teenpower Fullpower International® www.kidpower.org
© 2017 For permission to copy, contact safety@kidpower.org

IT'S YOUR FAULT! I WISH YOU'D NEVER BEEN BORN!
IT'S YOUR FAULT! I WISH YOU'D NEVER BEEN BORN!
IT'S YOUR FAULT! I WISH YOU'D NEVER BEEN BORN!
IT'S YOUR FAULT! I WISH YOU'D NEVER BEEN BORN!

4. Mike dreams all night about the fight and the mean things his mother said.

A publication of Kidpower Teenpower Fullpower International® www.kidpower.org
© 2017 For permission to copy, contact safety@kidpower.org

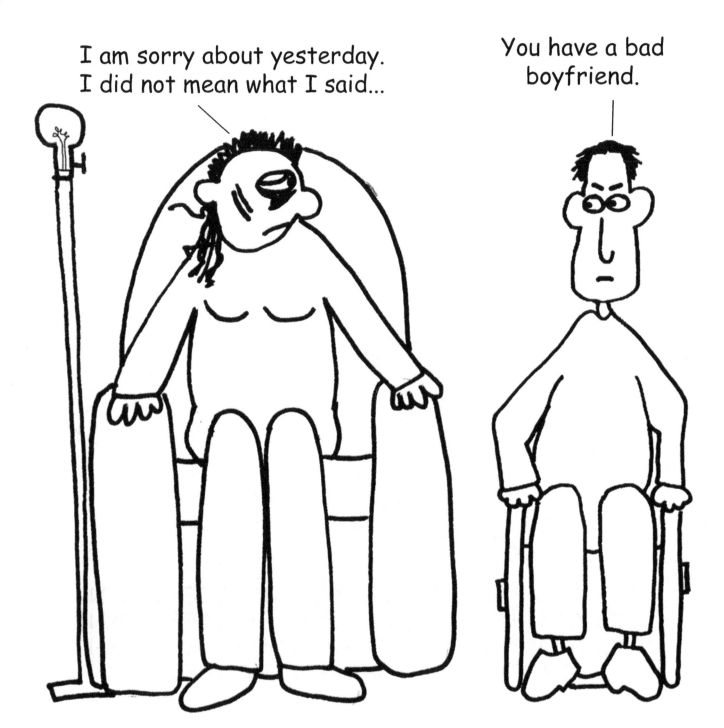

5. In the morning, Mike's mother is sorry. He is upset.

A publication of Kidpower Teenpower Fullpower International® www.kidpower.org
© 2017 For permission to copy, contact safety@kidpower.org

6. Mike tells his friends about his problem. His friends give him good advice.

To Practice

SAY: Get help.

DO: Remember that when others fight, it is not your fault.

A publication of Kidpower Teenpower Fullpower International® www.kidpower.org
© 2017 For permission to copy, contact safety@kidpower.org

It is not your fault when your mother and her boyfriend fight. But you cannot make your mother change boyfriends. We can think about another place for you to live. Or you can make a Safety Plan for when fights happen.

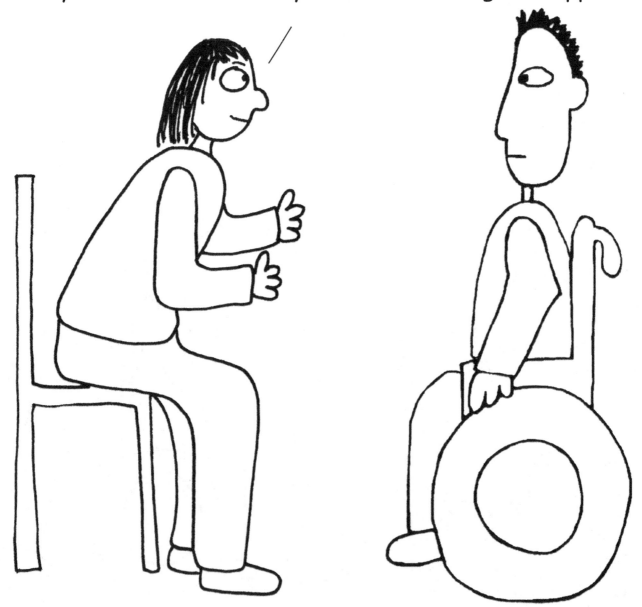

7. Mike talks to a counselor. She tells Mike about his different choices.

To Practice
SAY : Make a Safety Plan.

A publication of Kidpower Teenpower Fullpower International® www.kidpower.org
© 2017 For permission to copy, contact safety@kidpower.org

8. Next time there is a fight, Mike goes to his room. He knows now that if he thinks someone might get hurt, his safety plan is to call 911.

Mei Lin Has A Problem Boyfriend

1. Mei Lin gets tired and wants to leave the party early. Her boyfriend gets mad at her.

A publication of Kidpower Teenpower Fullpower International® www.kidpower.org

2. Mei Lin's boyfriend gets jealous. This makes Mei Lin mad. It is NOT loving to be jealous or insulting — or to hit, push, or grab.

A publication of Kidpower Teenpower Fullpower International® www.kidpower.org
© 2017 For permission to copy, contact safety@kidpower.org

3. Mei Lin's boyfriend pushes her and says mean things. She tells him she wants to go away from him.

To Practice

DO: Take a step back to find your balance. Use a strong, firm voice.

SAY: STOP! I AM LEAVING!

A publication of Kidpower Teenpower Fullpower International® www.kidpower.org
© 2017 For permission to copy, contact safety@kidpower.org

4. Mei Lin's boyfriend grabs her arm hard. It hurts. He says that she cannot leave.

A publication of Kidpower Teenpower Fullpower International®   www.kidpower.org
© 2017 For permission to copy, contact safety@kidpower.org

5. Mei Lin pulls her arm away and yells for help.

To Practice

DO: Grab your own hand and pull your arm away with your whole body and voice.

SAY: Yell 'NO! HELP!'

6. Mei Lin is sad. Her boyfriend is mad. Her friends want to help.

To Practice

SAY: Get help.

A publication of Kidpower Teenpower Fullpower International®   www.kidpower.org
© 2017 For permission to copy, contact safety@kidpower.org

7. Mei Lin's boyfriend goes away.

I am sad about my boyfriend. He was really nice when he wasn't in a bad mood.

You deserve a better guy!

I know you miss him, but your boyfriend should respect you all the time.

It is not safe to have a boyfriend who tries to hit or grab you.

8. Mei Lin misses her boyfriend. Her friends tell her that she needs a better boyfriend.

To Practice

SAY: True couples do not force each other to do things they don't want.

A publication of Kidpower Teenpower Fullpower International® www.kidpower.org
© 2017 For permission to copy, contact safety@kidpower.org

9. Mei Lin meets a new guy. He is really nice. When she wants to go home, he listens.

Mei Lin Uses An Emergency Lie

I miss you so much. I think about you all the time. I am sorry I hurt you. Don't you care about me?

I HATE HIM. But I do not feel safe telling him this.

1. Most of the time we want to keep our promises and tell the truth. But you do not have to keep your promises or tell the truth to someone who is threatening you with violence.

To Practice

DO: Squeeze your lips together to remember your Mouth Closed Power.

A publication of Kidpower Teenpower Fullpower International® www.kidpower.org
© 2017 For permission to copy, contact safety@kidpower.org

2. Your job is to get away from that person as soon as you can and report what happened to someone who can help you.

To Practice

DO: Use a calm, firm voice.

SAY: My friend will be back soon. I'll call you later.

DO: Get help as soon as you safely can.

A publication of Kidpower Teenpower Fullpower International® www.kidpower.org
© 2017 For permission to copy, contact safety@kidpower.org

Mike Protects His Feelings At The Dance

1. Mike goes with his friends to the dance. He sees a beautiful woman in a beautiful dress. He thinks he is falling in love. Mei Lin tells him to go ask the woman for a dance.

2. Mike asks the beautiful woman for a dance. She is mean. She is NOT acting beautiful even if she looks beautiful.

To Practice

DO: Be ready to hear the answer 'No'.

SAY: Would you like to dance?

SAY: No, thank you.

SAY: OK.

158

3. Mike's friends help him to throw away the mean words the woman said. Mike takes their nice words inside his heart.

To Practice
DO: Throw away the words "You can't dance!"
SAY: Dancing is for everyone to enjoy!

A publication of Kidpower Teenpower Fullpower International® www.kidpower.org
© 2017 For permission to copy, contact safety@kidpower.org

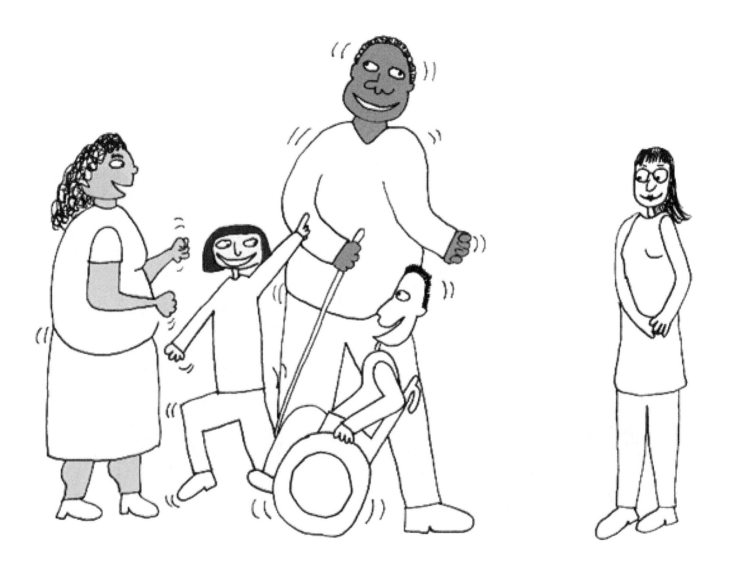

4. Mike and his friends have fun dancing together. A nice woman watches them. She is a little shy.

A publication of Kidpower Teenpower Fullpower International® www.kidpower.org
© 2017 For permission to copy, contact safety@kidpower.org

5. Mike asks the shy woman to dance.

To Practice

DO: Be ready to hear the answer 'No'.

SAY: Would you like to dance?

SAY: I'd love to.

SAY: Great!

A publication of Kidpower Teenpower Fullpower International® www.kidpower.org
© 2017 For permission to copy, contact safety@kidpower.org

6. Everybody has a wonderful time at the dance.

Fullpower Means: Put Safety First!
Put Safety First by paying attention, speaking up, moving away from trouble, and getting help.

1. Safety First means telling people when they hurt your feelings.

2. Safety First means walking away from trouble even when someone is rude.

3. Safety First means using your awareness both to enjoy the world and to watch out for trouble.

4. Safety First means noticing when a fight is about to happen.

5. Safety First means reporting a problem even if you are embarrassed.

163

A publication of Kidpower Teenpower Fullpower International® www.kidpower.org

Kidpower Protection Promise™
For All Ages And Abilities Everywhere

Imagine the impact if we each discussed this message with everyone who is important in our lives—and convinced them that we mean it!

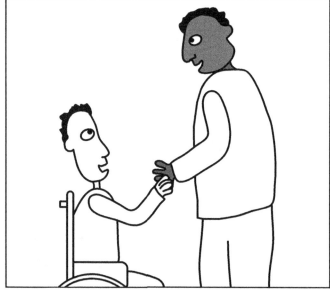

"You are VERY important to me! If you have a safety problem, I want to know. Even if I seem too busy. Or might feel upset. Or don't understand at first. Even if someone we care about will be upset. Even if it is embarrassing. Even if you made a mistake or promised not to tell. Please tell me, and I will do everything in my power to help you."

A publication of Kidpower Teenpower Fullpower International® www.kidpower.org
© 2017 For permission to copy, contact safety@kidpower.org

Kidpower Services For All Ages and Abilities

Overview

Kidpower Teenpower Fullpower International is a global nonprofit leader dedicated to providing effective and empowering child protection, positive communication, and personal safety skills for all ages and abilities. Since 1989, Kidpower has served over 4.4 million children, teenagers, and adults, including those with difficult life challenges, locally and around the world through our in-person workshops, educational resources, and partnerships. We give our students the opportunity for successful practice of 'People Safety' skills in ways that help prepare them to develop healthy relationships, increase their confidence, take charge of their emotional and physical safety, and act safely and respectfully towards others.

For more information, visit kidpower.org or contact safety@kidpower.org.

Workshops

Through our centers and travelling instructors, Kidpower has led workshops in over 60 countries spanning six continents. Our programs include: Parent/Caregiver seminars; Parent-Child workshops; training for educators and other professionals; classroom workshops; Family workshops; Teenpower self-defense workshops for teens; Collegepower for young people leaving home; Fullpower self-defense and boundary-setting workshops for adults; Seniorpower for older people; adapted programs for people with special needs; and workplace safety, communication, and team-building seminars. Our three-day Child Protection Advocates Training Institute prepares educators and other professionals, as well as parents and other caring adults, to use Kidpower's intervention, advocacy, and personal safety skills in their personal and professional lives.

Online Library

Our extensive online Library provides over 200 free 'People Safety' resources including articles, videos, webinars, blogs, and podcasts. Free downloads for individual use are available of online publications like our Kidpower Safety Signs, coloring book, and handouts. We provide licensing for use of materials or content for charitable and educational purposes.

Books

We publish an extensive preschool through high school curriculum, as well as books about personal safety for adults. (Please visit our website bookstore for a complete list):

* *The Kidpower Book for Caring Adults:*
  Personal Safety, Self-Protection, Confidence, and Advocacy for Young People
* Cartoon-illustrated *Safety Comics* and *Teaching Books* for children, teens, and adults
* *Bullying; What Adults Need to Know and Do to Keep Kids Safe*
* *Fullpower Relationship Safety Skills Handbook for Teens and Adults*
* *One Strong Move: Cartoon-Illustrated Self-defense Lessons*
* *Earliest Teachable Moment: Personal Safety for Babies, Toddlers, and Preschoolers*
* *Face Bullying with Confidence: Creating Cultures of Respect and Safety for All Ages and Stages of Life*

Coaching, Consulting, and Curriculum Development

Long-distance coaching by video-conferencing, telephone, and e-mail enables us to make our services accessible worldwide. We consult with a wide range of experts, organizations, and schools on how best to adapt our program to meet unserved needs and develop new curriculum to increase the 'People Safety' knowledge for different people facing difficult life challenges.

Instructor Training and Center Development

Our very comprehensive certified instructor training program prepares qualified people to teach our programs and to establish centers and offices for organizing services in their communities under our organizational umbrella.

A publication of Kidpower Teenpower Fullpower International® www.kidpower.org

Acknowledgements

Kidpower is a tapestry of many different threads woven by many different hands. Our curriculum has grown from the ideas, questions, teaching, feedback, and stories of countless people since I first started working on child protection, personal safety, and self-defense issues in 1985.

I want to express my appreciation to each of our Kidpower instructors, board members, honorary trustees, senior program leaders, center directors, workshop organizers, advisors, volunteers, donors, parents, students, funding partners, service partners, family members, advocates, hosts, and office staff.

Thank you for the thought, care, time, and generosity that you have given to bring Kidpower Teenpower Fullpower International to where we are today. I feel honored to have you as colleagues and as friends.

Writing each person's story would be a book unto itself. You can learn about the remarkable people who have built and keep building our organization by reading *A Tapestry Woven By Many Different Hands* on our website.

I want to give special acknowledgement to people who have helped to create our cartoon-illustrated Safety Comics and Teaching Books series in many different ways.

Amanda Golert is a Senior Program Leader, Training and Curriculum Consultant, and our Sweden Center Director since 1999. Amanda's role has been crucial in the development of all of our cartoon-illustrated books as the artist, designer, and primary editor.

Our Montreal Center Director, School Implementation Project Coordinator, and Senior Program **Marylaine Léger** has provided major editing, re-organizing, and re-formatting for all the skill sets in this book.

Timothy Dunphy, our Program Co-Founder, worked with me for many years to create our curriculum and still teaches and serves as a member of our training team.

Senior Program Leader **Chantal Keeney** provided major help with editing, teaching instructions, and content development of our original cartoon-illustrated curriculum.

Our California Program Director **Erika Leonard**; New Zealand Center Co-Director **Cornelia Baumgartner**; Colorado Springs Center Director **Jan Isaacs Henry**; and Chicago Center Director **Joe Connelly**, who also are all Senior Program Leaders, have each contributed important ideas and improvements to these Kidpower social stories, explanations, and skills over the years.

Finally, thank you to Kidpower Instructor and Senior Program Leader **John Luna-Sparks**, LCSW, CMP, for many years of support, including working with me to create our original Safety Signals.

About The Author

Irene van der Zande is the executive director, founder and primary author for Kidpower Teenpower Fullpower International. Since Kidpower was established in 1989, Irene has led the development of the organization's services, the creation of the curriculum, the establishment of centers, and the training of instructors. Her inspiration for starting Kidpower came from an experience in 1985, when she protected a group of young children, including her own two, from a man threatening to kidnap them.

Irene is an internationally recognized expert on designing, implementing, and teaching programs that help to protect kids, teens, and adults, including those with special needs, from bullying, abuse, harassment, domestic and relationship violence, assault, and abduction - and that also prepare them to become stronger leaders, increase their confidence, and develop healthy relationships that add joy and meaning to their lives.

Prior to starting Kidpower, Irene was a community organizer and author. Her first book *1, 2, 3 ... The Toddler Years* is still used in child development programs in colleges and preschools. Since then, she has published numerous articles, books, videos, and other educational materials about her work.

About The Illustrator

Amanda Golert is an experienced self-defense instructor, trainer, passionate advocate for empowerment and safety of children and other vulnerable people, the Center Director of Kidpower Sweden—and she also likes to draw!

Since 1999, Amanda has supported the growth and development of Kidpower Teenpower Fullpower International. She works in partnership with Irene to illustrate, edit, and design the Kidpower cartoon books and many other educational materials. The results of her work provide effective tools worldwide for educators and other professionals as well as parents and other caring adults who want to learn and teach child protection, self-defense, and 'People Safety' strategies and skills.

About The Editor

Marylaine Léger has been teaching self-defense and empowerment skills to people of all ages and abilities since 1992. Since 1996, she has been leading our Kidpower Montreal Center as well as providing support to the training and program development for our international organization. She is deeply committed to bringing Kidpower to everyone, everywhere.

In 2015, she became the coordinator of our School Implementation Task Force. She took on the challenge of adapting our curriculum into a twelve-lesson format, more accessible to classroom teachers, and provided extensive organizing and editing for this book.

A publication of Kidpower Teenpower Fullpower International® www.kidpower.org
© 2017 For permission to copy, contact safety@kidpower.org

Made in the USA
Middletown, DE
15 October 2021